The Appalachian Trail

For Morgan, welcome to the family! —M. D. B.

To Sabrena —J. G. W.

SIMON SPOTLIGHT
An imprint of Simon & Schuster Children's Publishing Division
1230 Avenue of the Americas, New York, New York 10020
This Simon Spotlight edition May 2020

For information about special discounts for bulk purchases, please contact
Simon & Schuster Special Sales at 1-866-506-1949 or
business@simonandschuster.com.
Manufactured in the United States of America 0420 LAK
2 4 6 8 10 9 7 5 3 1
Library of Congress Cataloging-in-Publication Data
Names: Bauer, Marion Dane, author. | Wallace, John, 1966– illustrator.
Title: The Appalachian Trail / by Marion Dane Bauer ;
illustrated by John Wallace.
Description: New York : Simon Spotlight, An imprint of Simon & Schuster
Children's Publishing Division, 2020. | Series: Ready-to-read | Audience:
Grades K–1 | Audience: Ages 4–6 | Summary: "With her trademark simple
but lyrical text enhanced by John Wallace's irresistible illustrations, Marion
Dane Bauer describes the wonders of the Appalachian Trail for Level One
beginning readers"—Provided by publisher.
Identifiers: LCCN 2019036181 | ISBN 9781534464582 (paperback) | ISBN
9781534464599 (hardcover) | ISBN 9781534464605 (eBook)
Subjects: LCSH: Appalachian Trail—Juvenile literature.
Classification: LCC F106 .B38 2020 | DDC 974—dc23
LC record available at https://lccn.loc.gov/2019036181

The Appalachian Trail

By Marion Dane Bauer

Illustrated by John Wallace

Ready-to-Read

SIMON SPOTLIGHT
New York London Toronto Sydney New Delhi

Do you like to hike?

Can you imagine hiking for 2,192 miles?

The Appalachian
(say: Appa-LATCH-uhn)
Trail (or AT, for short)
is that long!

Springer
Mountain

It stretches between
Springer Mountain in Georgia
and Mount Katahdin
(say: ka-TAH-din) in Maine.

Each year thousands
of people set out
to through-hike the AT.
That means to hike it
from end to end.

A through-hike
of the AT
takes around
five to seven months
to complete.

Only about one in four
people make it the whole way.

About three million
people walk part
of the trail each year.

The AT is one of the longest footpaths in the world.
It stretches through fourteen states.

White paint marks lead the way.

Hikers go up and down mountains.

Hikers cross rivers and valleys.

Through-hikers carry tents.
Or they sleep in huts
at night.

They pick up supplies like
water and food in nearby
towns.
Then they return to
hiking.

At different points
hikers might see eagles,
turkeys, moose, and deer.

Sometimes they even see shy animals like black bears and bobcats. Mice may visit their camps at night.

The AT is rich in trees and flowers, in sunrises and sunsets.

And in changing weather!

This is all part of the wilderness.

The wilderness can test us and teach us.

We must take care of our wild places so others can enjoy them too.

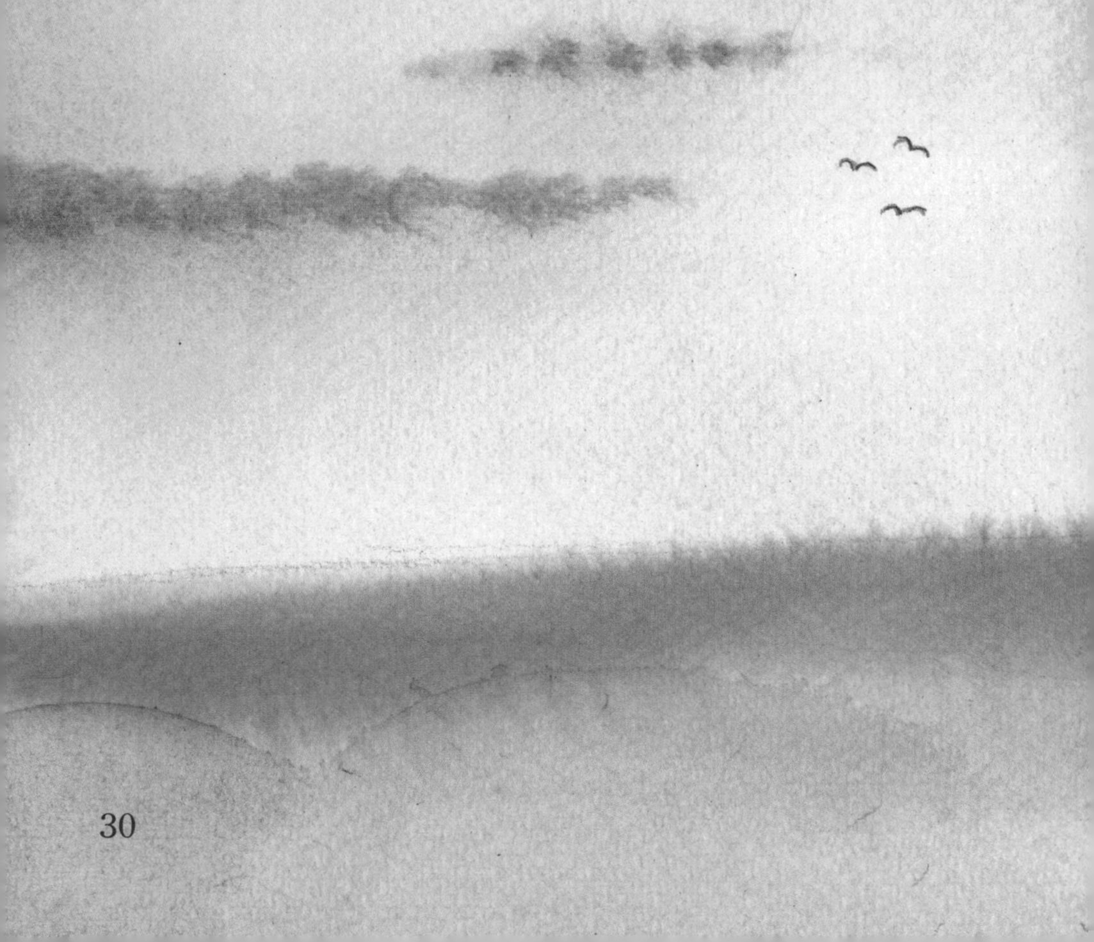

We are lucky to have the
Appalachian Trail!

Interesting facts about the Appalachian Trail

★ The Appalachian Mountain Range is thought to be one of the oldest mountain ranges in the world. It existed even before the North American continent came into being. These mountains were once as tall as the Alps or the Rocky Mountains.

★ About one hundred years ago, a man named Benton MacKaye came up with the idea for the Appalachian Trail. He worked to make it become real, too. He wanted Americans to renew their spirits in nature.

★ Emma Gatewood, nicknamed on the AT as Grandma Gatewood, was the first woman to hike the entire Appalachian Trail alone. She was more than sixty-five years old when she did it. She was also the first person, man or woman, to walk it more than once.

★ The Appalachian Trail connects fourteen states. They are Georgia, North Carolina, Tennessee, Virginia, West Virginia, Maryland, Pennsylvania, New Jersey, New York, Connecticut, Massachusetts, Vermont, New Hampshire, and Maine.

★ While most of the AT is wilderness, several sections pass right through towns.

★ More than 20,000 hikers have completed the entire Appalachian Trail.